For my family. I love you all so much.

–T.P.

www.theenglishschoolhouse.com

ISBN: 978-1-955130-01-1

Black is More than Just a Color

By Dr. Tamara Pizzoli • Art by Shai Digital

Black is a blessing,

and a
beat.

and a
feeling,

and a
poem.

Black is a rhythm,

and an
understanding.

It is
a lineage.

It is a love.

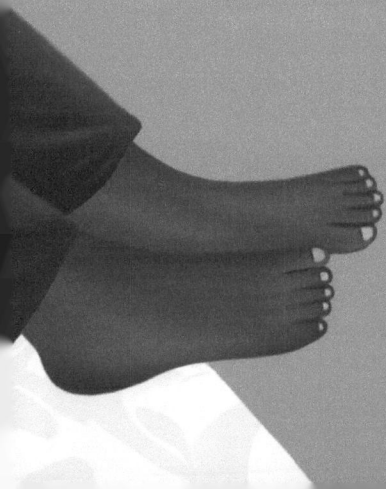

Black is a song,

and a spectrum,

and a knowing.

Black is a community, a connection,

and
a code.

Black is a gift,
and a wonder,
and a truth.

Black is history.
Black is now.
Black is future.

www.ingramcontent.com/pod-product-compliance
Lightning Source LLC
Chambersburg PA
CBHW060825090426
42738CB00003B/106